FAITHFUL
yet CHANGING

FAITHFUL
yet CHANGING

THE CHURCH *in*
CHALLENGING TIMES

BISHOP MARK S. HANSON

Augsburg Books
MINNEAPOLIS

FAITHFUL YET CHANGING
The Church in Challenging Times

Large-quantity purchases or custom editions of this book are available at a discount from the publisher. For more information, contact the sales department at Augsburg Fortress, Publishers, 1-800-328-4648, or write to: Sales Director, Augsburg Fortress, Publishers, P.O. Box 1209, Minneapolis, MN 55440-1209.

Scripture quotations are from the New Revised Standard Version Bible, copyright © 1989 by the Division of Christian Education of the National Council of the Churches of Christ in the U.S.A. and used by permission.

Some of the material in this book was adapted from articles in *The Lutheran Magazine* © Augsburg Fortress, Publishers. Dec 2001 issue, p. 61, "Come, Lord Jesus" by Mark S. Hanson and January 2002 issue, p. 53, "First Impressions" by Mark S. Hanson.

Excerpts marked LBW are from *Lutheran Book of Worship,* copyright © 1978.

Excerpts marked WOV are from *With One Voice: A Lutheran Resource for Worship* (Minneapolis: Augsburg Fortress, 1995).

Cover and book design by Michelle L. N. Cook
Cover photo by Michael D. Watson, *The Lutheran Magazine*

ISBN 0-8066-4474-5

The paper used in this publication meets the minimum requirements of American National Standard for Information Sciences—Permanence of Paper for Printed Library Materials, ANSI Z329.48-1984.

Manufactured in the U.S.A.   AF 9-4474

06   05   04   03   02   4   5   6   7   8   9   10

CONTENTS

INTRODUCTION

I have a passion for the gospel of Jesus Christ, a love for the people of God, and an ache for the brokenness of the world.

What I am hearing in the Evangelical Lutheran Church in America is that this church wants a bishop who will articulate the mission, rooted in word and sacrament, to which God is calling us—and help us imagine what the church can look like for the sake of mission. In these challenging times, we seek together to be a church that is faithful yet changing.

I come with more questions than answers. An anxious church dwells on what it lacks, seems hopelessly divided, and becomes distrustful of its leaders. In an anxious church, members and congregations begin to distance themselves from the larger church.

- Is the ELCA in a state of anxiety, or does it have a sense of urgency for mission?
- Do we share a sense of urgency for equipping every member of every ELCA congregation to be a witness?
- Do we share a sense of urgency for starting new congregations in those fast-growing

areas of our country where we are not now present?

• Are we ready to expand our ministry with the new immigrants in our communities?

• Do we share a sense of urgency for increasing our support of the ELCA World Hunger Appeal and the Stand with Africa campaign?

• Are we ready to dig down deep into the root causes of poverty until, as Kathryn Wolford of Lutheran World Relief says, "Every one of us has calluses on our hands"?

• Do we share a sense of urgency for healing the deep divisions in this church?

• Can we be a church with a sense of urgency for God's mission, yet avoid becoming so frenetic with activity that we forget this is the Lord's church, not ours, and that we live each day bathed in God's grace, marked with the cross of Christ, and sealed with the Holy Spirit forever?

My hope is that I can invite this church into a time of prayer, lively conversation, and holy imagination regarding what God can do when the members of eleven thousand congregations are joined in mission in Christ's name. This strategic planning process will involve congregational members, synod assemblies, the ELCA Church Council, the Conference of Bishops, the ELCA churchwide staff, church-related institutions, and the 2003 churchwide assembly. I trust that this process will give focus and commitment to our shared mission as the Evangelical Lutheran Church in America.

I have been asked to share my vision for the ELCA. I do so mindful that we have called this whole church into a time of strategic thinking and planning regarding our future. In this little book I share that vision. I see us as:

a witnessing church,
a worshiping church,
an engaging church,
an equipping church,
an inviting church,
a connecting church,
a changing church,
a praying church.

My hope is that in every congregation in the ELCA a group of Christians will gather around these themes for conversation and prayer, to seek together to clarify a vision of what this church might be in mission.

My thanks to Marvin Roloff, CEO of Augsburg Fortress, Publishers, for asking me to write this book. Thanks to Ron Klug for engaging me in conversation, providing editorial assistance, and writing the discussion questions and worship suggestions. My thanks to all the people who have shared their faith stories with me and with you.

I continue to give thanks to God for the memory of my parents, Oscar and Myrtle Hanson, and for my father-in-law, J. Elmo Agrimson, and for the continued witness of my mother-in-law, Cordelia Agrimson. Their living faith, their love for the church, and their wisdom and courage shape my leadership. For the deep love I share with Ione and for her poetic and empathetic listening, I give thanks to God. Our children—Aaron, Alyssa, Rachel, Ezra, Isaac, and Elizabeth—and granddaughter Naomi remind me daily of the resiliency of God's grace and the joys and challenges of living in an inclusive world.

My prayers are with all who read this book as we seek together to discern the mission to which God invites us. What a holy calling it is that we share!

—Mark S. Hanson, Presiding Bishop
Evangelical Lutheran Church in America

Chapter 1

A WITNESSING
CHURCH

When I first met with the churchwide staff, all five hundred in small groups, I asked each person—computer technicians, executive assistants, bookkeepers, unit executives—to share one sign of God at work in their lives, in their work, their families, the world. In every meeting, at first there was quiet, then there were incredibly moving stories, tearful stories, hopeful stories.

One woman began crying and said, "A sign of God at work is that I'm here today. Eight months ago I went home from work intending to take my life, because I had to make the decision to terminate life support for my forty-two-year-old brother. I felt so guilty and so empty and so responsible that I saw no way out except to join him in death. I had the bottle of pills ready, but I couldn't do it.

"Yesterday I received a letter from the organ donor agency that received his organs, telling me about the people who were alive because of that gift. This gave some meaning to my brother's death." She began to talk about a God who sustained her in her grief and how she understands anew what it means to believe in the resurrection from the dead.

Another person said, "A sign of God at work is that you are here and asked this question. On Friday I'm having an angiogram, and I'm terrified. I haven't known how to talk with my colleagues about this, but now your question has opened the way for me. I see that as a sign of God at work."

As a synod bishop, every time I visited a congregation and met with a church council or staff, I asked members to share signs that God is at work with people in that place, in the ministry of that congregation. Congregations, specialized ministries, synods, and churchwide staff all need to be communities of discernment, learning together to recognize the signs of God at work in our midst. Then we need to be a witnessing church in which every member is willing to tell about God at work in them and around them.

Shortly after Jesus' resurrection, his disciples asked him a searching question: "Lord, is this the time when you will restore the kingdom?" (Acts 1:6). Jesus answered, "It is not for you to know. . . . But you will receive power when the Holy Spirit has come upon you; and you will be my witnesses."

Witnessing is pointing to what God is doing. So we ask those confirming their faith in the Affirmation of Baptism: "Do you intend to continue in the covenant God made with you in Holy Baptism . . . to proclaim the good news of God in Christ through word and deed, to serve all people . . . to strive for justice and peace in all the earth?" Witnessing belongs to the vocation of all the baptized.

How can we help but witness? Think of how easily we share stories and pictures of grandchildren. Think of the impact of 5.1 million ELCA members who, like Peter and John, "cannot keep from speaking about what we have seen and heard" (Acts 4:20).

Witnessing begins in worship. There we behold Christ present in word and sacrament. There we experience the Spirit's power as people come to faith, as sins are forgiven, as the alienated are reconciled. How can we discern signs of God at work in our lives and the world if we don't immerse ourselves in the biblical story? Drawing on the Bible, the creeds, the Lutheran confessions, we witness to the creating, sustaining, redeeming, reconciling, sanctifying, and empowering work of the triune God.

Witnessing isn't a technique we learn. It belongs to the fabric of the Christian life. It begins in our homes as we talk about where we have experienced God's mercy and grace each day. Witnessing is both a public act and very personal. It involves speaking out for justice, working for peace, and listening to the anguished pleas of one who is depressed.

Witnessing is both individual and corporate. The civil rights movement in the United States in the 1960s and the struggle to end apartheid in South Africa happened in large part because of the public witness of people of faith.

Witnessing is born out of prayer. It is being open to God's work and the Spirit's power. Now, more than ever, the world needs our witness.

Bishop Hanson, where have you seen the signs of God active in your life lately?
For me, as for most of us, the clarity of God at work comes in hindsight rather than in the

moment. Last summer, for example, I had planned a sabbatical that was going to be an academic exploration of theological ideas, and somehow that became instead a time of returning to some sabbath rhythms, grounding life in prayer, relaxation, and walking. I returned to the country graveyards where my ancestors are buried, to the farm where my father was born. There I was surrounded by the saints and touched the roots of faith that have been so important to my life. I didn't know it at the time, but God was at work in these decisions. Now I see all this as preparation for this present call.

Also in our family we have had our share of struggles and painful moments. The fact that we are a family with deep bonds of love, living in the forgiveness of God that comes to us and through us to each other is a sign of God at work in my life.

How can people discern the presence of God in their lives?

Maybe I'm biased because I'm a strong extrovert, but I think it's a communal discipline. I need the insight of others to see what God is doing. What if every meeting in a congregation began by asking "Where *did* we experience

God in worship last Sunday? Where did we see God active during the week?" Asking the question, "Where is God?" can get us back into God's word in new ways.

Why is the term witnessing *a turn off for many?*

We associate witnessing with a kind of intimidating, interrogating, guilt-producing activity, trying to shame people into the kingdom of God. This is not the way Jesus invited people into life with God.

When people hear the word *witness* they often have images of being questioned by a prosecuting attorney or a defense attorney. They're afraid they will be asked questions they can't answer. But witnesses in a courtroom simply speak the truth about their experiences, what they have seen and heard. It is the same for witnesses in the church.

We may also resist witnessing, knowing it can be a costly activity, leading to rejection and even death, as it did for the martyrs of the early church, Dietrich Bonhoeffer in the twentieth century, or countless Christian martyrs in our own time. We need boldness and courage to witness, and that is born of the Holy Spirit.

Why do we have little trouble witnessing about our favorite sports team or a new grandchild, yet have a harder time witnessing about the Christian faith?

In part we have bought the cultural myth that faith is a private matter: you have yours and I have mine and we'll just tolerate our differences. In order to be inoffensive, we don't get around to talking about what really matters to us.

We also may fear that we won't say the right things. We have a perfectionist approach to witnessing, even though the Bible shows people struggling, lamenting God's absence. We don't have to have all the answers. It's all right if we share our doubts and questions.

When I was pastor of University Lutheran Church of Hope in Minneapolis, a member of the church committed suicide. That event elicited from the congregation stories of depression and suicide attempts, helping the whole congregation to ask, "How do we, as a community of faith, keep faith alive for those for whom God seems starkly absent?"

What right do I have to witness to people of another faith?

We don't need to say: "I'll keep my faith to myself if you keep yours to yourself." We can be open to hear one another's stories, to hear what is centrally orienting in another's life, to learn, for example, what it means to be a Muslim or Buddhist.

I can even be open to the possibility that God is at work in the faith of another in ways in which God is not yet at work in my life. The challenge is to be open to learning from one another without diminishing our own devotion to Christ, our commitment to the Christian faith, or our inviting people to hear the story of Jesus.

QUESTIONS FOR DISCUSSION

If your group has not had time to read the chapter beforehand, give them some time to read it silently now, or have it read aloud. Discuss the following questions. If your group is large, you may want to break up into threes or fours for at least some of the discussion.

1. Where do you see God active in your life, your congregation, your community?

2. Read Acts 1:1-11. What does it mean for you that Jesus said, "You will be my witnesses"?

3. Who are the people who most clearly and effectively witnessed to the Christian faith in your life? How did they do it?

4. What has been your most satisfying experience in Christian witnessing? the most frustrating?

5. What prevents you from being a more bold and active witness for God?

6. What would help you become a stronger witness for God? How might your congregation help?

7. What did you find most interesting and helpful in this chapter?

You may wish to celebrate your discussion by singing a hymn like one of the following:
LBW 381. "Hark, the Voice of Jesus Calling"
LBW 385. "What Wondrous Love Is This"
LBW 393. "Rise, Shine, You People!"
WOV 722. "Hallelujah! We Sing Your Praises"
WOV 753. "You Are the Seed"

Close with this or another prayer:
Lord God of our salvation, it is your will that all people might come to you through your

Son Jesus Christ. Inspire our witness to him, that all may know the power of his forgiveness and the hope of his resurrection. We pray in his name (LBW, p. 46).

Chapter 2

A WORSHIPING CHURCH

Witnessing means pointing to signs of God at work in our lives and in the world. Discerning God's activity is not always an easy task. Yet we believe there is one place God will be present: that is in the community gathered in Christ for worship.

In worship God is present through God's living word of promise—"in the mercy of Almighty God, Jesus Christ was given to die for you, and for his sake God forgives you all your sins." In worship Christ is present for you: "Take and eat; this is my body given for you . . . this cup is the new covenant in my blood, shed for you and for all people for the forgiveness of sin."

At the heart of Lutheran worship is God's grace—heard in the proclamation of the word, received in the meal of Christ's presence, given in the waters of Baptism. In worship we experience both the mystery and majesty of God's transcendence and the intimacy of God's loving presence. It is here that our hearts are filled with joy as we praise God with music and "speak to one another with psalms, hymns, and spiritual songs" (Eph. 5:19). In the gathered community the Holy Spirit works through the gospel. Lives are being changed; sins are being forgiven; those who feel less than human are being restored to full humanity; faith is professed; broken families are reconciled.

I remember one woman in our parish who was struggling with breast cancer. She was often so weary from the treatments that some days she'd come to the church, sit in a chair by the baptismal font, letting her hands rest in the waters, being reminded of the refreshment of God's grace. She remembered how at the beginning of her life she was given the promise that her life was in God for eternity. The font was the most refreshing and renewing place she could put herself, literally back in the waters of Baptism.

We sometimes forget how startling are the acts we perform, the words we hear, the faith we confess. Why is it that only thirty percent of ELCA members gather for worship on any Sunday morning?

Is it that we have become consumers, viewing worship as one choice among many on a Sunday morning? Maybe familiarity breeds complacency. In worship we are standing in Christ before the throne of grace, interceding for the world, hearing God's liberating word for us and the whole creation, being fed by Christ's presence and sent out to serve. This is the central event in our lives of faith.

In our worship we need to keep one thing central—the gospel in word and sacrament. We can then be imaginative about all the other things—the beat of our songs, the language of our proclamation, the words of our prayers. We can be creative and diverse as long as the means of grace remain central.

How can we talk about grace so people can really understand and experience it?

Joseph Sittler wrote in *Gravity and Grace:* "The grace of God is not simply a holy hypodermic whereby my sins are forgiven. It is the whole giftedness of life, the wonder of life, which causes me to ask questions that transcend the moment" (p. 14). We need to find rich ways of talking about and experiencing the liberating grace of God.

It seems people today have a greater desire to experience God in worship than to have God explained. That is a challenge for Lutherans who have been suspicious of subjective experience. We emphasize the external word, the revealed word, clung to by faith. Is the idea of experience inconsistent with that understanding?

When I have asked people to name where they experience God active in their lives, many said, "I've been given this day of life." That's basic: this day of new life is a gift of God's grace.

I remember Gerhard Frost once saying that grace is God's gift of the freedom to live with incompleteness. I never have to do it all. This is a word of good news for people whose "To Do" lists grow longer every day.

There are people whose issue is not guilt but shame, not arrogance but feeling less than human. They're not looking for freedom from guilt but a word that says they are a new creation, a human being capable of loving and being loved. The word of grace for them is: "in Christ, you are of infinite worth."

Everywhere we go we have to prove our worthiness. At the bank I have to prove I'm worthy to get a loan. At the airport I have to prove I'm worthy to get on the plane. Church should be the one place where my acceptance and worthiness is not dependent on anything I have to call forth from myself. It is God's radical gift in Christ that makes me a new creation, unconditionally loved. By the Holy Spirit I lay hold of God's claim on me in faith.

Is the preferred member of your congregation the person who fits the profile of Jesus' beatitudes (the poor, the hungry, those who weep)? Or those Paul mentions in 1 Corinthians 1 (the foolish, the weak, the low, and the despised)? Why do so many who fit those descriptions feel unwanted and unwelcome in worship? Do we forget that Luther reminds us that we all come before God's mercy seat as beggars?

I wonder if preachers should declare a one-year moratorium on using the word "gospel" in sermons. It has become an insider word that has meaning for some but not for all. Rather than use that shorthand word, would it not be better to hear the good news spoken clearly, such as, "God in Christ loves you, forgives you, frees you"? Can we do any better than Paul? "So if anyone is in Christ, there is a new creation: everything old has passed away; see, everything has become new!" (2 Cor. 5:17).

What do you mean when you talk about hearing the word?

The word of God is the revealed and written word in the Bible, but it should not be reduced to only that. It is the living word, incarnate in Christ, recorded in Scripture, proclaimed from the pulpit, and it is the word we speak to one another. I wish we could reclaim that fuller sense of the word of God.

One lay person said, "Every Sunday the pastor says, 'Go in peace. Serve the Lord.' But the next Sunday he never asks me how I did at it." Research shows that ninety-seven percent of ELCA churches include the Creeds in Sunday worship, but only three percent include sharing the stories of faith of God's people in that congregation. The word is not just the Scripture readings and sermon. It is the word we speak to one another, inside or outside the church walls, what Luther called "the mutual conversation and consolation" of brothers and sisters in Christ. I want to ask, "What would happen if we thought of ourselves as means of grace?"

How would you reply to the person who says, "I don't go to church because I just don't get much out of it"?

We are conditioned to be consumers, so it is natural for us to ask, "What do I get out of this?" But what if our first question was "What is God doing here? What did God get out of this? Was God glorified? How will God answer our intercessory prayers on behalf of the world?"

The church does not exist for its own sake but for the sake of the world. The church is not a port in a storm, but a vessel for carrying the gospel of God's love and grace on the tumultuous seas.

QUESTIONS FOR DISCUSSION

1. When you hear the word "grace," what images or words come to mind?

2. Read 2 Peter 3:18. How does God want you to grow in grace?

3. What do you appreciate most about the worship in your congregation?

4. What parts of the church service most clearly communicate grace to you?

5. What percentage of your congregation is present in weekly worship? What would have to change for that number to rise significantly?

6. Theologian Douglas John Hall speaks of the quest for mystery, for meaning, for the

presence of God, and for community. How are these quests being satisfied in your congregation's life? Where in the liturgy are they being satisfied?

7. What did you find most interesting or helpful in this chapter?

You may want to end your discussion by singing one of the following hymns:
LBW 245. "All People That on Earth Do Dwell"
LBW 257. "Holy Spirit, Truth Divine"
LBW 448. "Amazing Grace, How Sweet the Sound"
WOV 717. "Come, All You People"
WOV 719. "God Is Here!"

Close with this or another prayer:
O God, increase the faith and energy of your Church to desire and work for the salvation of all people, that they might be freed from sin and that hope be renewed in many hearts, to the increase of the kingdom of your Son, Jesus Christ our Lord (LBW, p. 45).

Chapter 3

AN ENGAGING CHURCH

In John 20, we read of the first Easter evening, when the disciples were huddled behind closed doors, terrified. Jesus, the risen Christ, stood among them and said, "As the Father has sent me, so I send you." They might have feared that they would be crucified, as Jesus had been. But he breathed on them and gave them a promise: "Receive the Holy Spirit." Like those first followers of Jesus, we are sent by God into the world as bearers of new life.

In the Affirmation of Baptism, we promise to gather with the people of God, hear the word, and share at the Lord's table. We go on to promise that in keeping the covenant God made with us in our baptism, we will also:

• proclaim the good news of God in Christ through word and deed,

• serve all people, following the example of our Lord Jesus,

• strive for justice and peace in all the earth.

I have asked confirmands to begin each day by putting their hands on their heads, recalling how water had been poured on them, saying, "I am baptized. I am chosen. I am a child of God. I belong to Jesus Christ," and then make the sign of the cross. That is a connecting link from the Sunday liturgy to the life of the faithful, and from the life of the faithful to the life of the world.

As people of faith, we are engaged in the world. This is not open to debate. But the nature of our involvement is always open to prayerful discernment. The challenge is to be in conversation with one another to know what response is called for in a given situation. I believe it is imperative that the poor and victims of injustice be full participants in those deliberations, because they are the very persons who are calling and leading the church into the world.

The world is God's creation and object of God's redemption in Christ, so we will be engaged in the world as stewards of the environment, as citizens and co-creators with God.

The world is also where evil exists, where the devil prowls seeking someone to devour, so we will be resistors, confronting evil in the world, casting it out in the name of the crucified Christ.

At the same time the world is not our home. We are sojourners, just passing through. We will always remain somewhat detached from the world, *in* the world but not *of* the world.

Our engagement in the world can be guided by the words of Eberhard Jüngel in his book *Justification: The Heart of the Christian Faith:* "For believers know that since God has done enough for our salvation, we can never do enough for the good of the world. So we are justified by faith alone, but faith never stays alone; it strives to, it has to become active in love; faith is never alone. There is no more liberating basis for ethics than the doctrine of justification of sinners by faith alone" (p. 259).

Our primary place of engagement in the world needs to be among the poor, because this is where God has said God will be. I am haunted by the Old Testament prophets who had the audacity to suggest that when God looks at the quality of our faith, God will look not at the eloquence of our preaching or the beauty of our sanctuaries, or the melodies of our songs, but at the condition of the poor in the land. On the basis of that, God will discern whether we have been faithful.

A year ago, for my devotional life, I read through the Bible in one year. It was a year in which we in the ELCA were struggling a lot about ecumenical agreements and human sexuality, but I kept noting all the Scripture passages calling for justice for the poor. If that is what so concerns God, why is this not the issue that agitates us and becomes the focus for our struggle? Might it possibly be true that the quality of life is not measured by Wall Street economic indicators but by the condition of the life of those who are poor?

Some of the most transforming moments in my life have occurred when I was engaged with people in poverty, in a very different context from my own, in which I had to listen to the stories of others and see myself through the eyes of another in Harlem, Chicago, inner-city Minneapolis, Mexico, Tanzania.

As I look around our church, I see a growing commitment to being a servant people. Youth and adults are working with Habitat for Humanity, providing food shelves, setting up homeless shelters, creating tutoring and recreation programs for neighborhood children.

How encouraging it is to see high school, college, and young adult groups on servant trips. They are leading this church in our commitment to ministry with those in poverty. These young people remind us that living the faith, learning the faith, and sharing the faith are inseparable.

While we serve others, we also need to talk more openly about power. Power is simply the ability to make something happen. It can be used for good or for evil. The risen Christ promised his disciples that they would receive power when the Holy Spirit came upon them and that they would be witnesses throughout the world (Acts 1:8).

How do we as people of faith exercise that power for the sake of justice and peace in the world? I have found those trained in congregation-based organizing to be enormously helpful in this regard. They help us claim the power we have when acting together in common cause. They teach us to be strategic in our actions. They challenge us not only to call forth leaders but to make sure those leaders have training—whether it be in confronting the changes in the rural economy and small towns or in the need to create metropolitan solutions to the disparities that exist in so many metropolitan communities. We can be more effective when we build strong community organizations. We have been given power to confront the principalities and powers.

As servants, we have a sense of compassion that leads us to acts of mercy *for* the poor. But we also need to listen *to* the poor, asking, "Why are people poor?" In striving for justice, we ask the deeper questions and dig deeper into the root causes of poverty.

To do this, our church must be made up of communities of moral deliberation and bold action. We will need to learn how to listen to those with whom we do not agree. Our deliberations must be grounded in Scripture and the Lutheran Confessions. In our deliberations, we will share our experiences and together discover the most effective ways to strive for peace and justice in all the earth.

What difference can I make in the world? I'm only one person.

That is precisely why it is so important that we are connected with others in the ELCA, with other Lutherans around the world, and with all Christians everywhere.

In our life together as the ELCA, we have many opportunities to serving all people and keep our baptismal covenant by striving for justice and peace. Take, for example, Stand with Africa, a three-year campaign of Lutheran World Relief, ELCA World Hunger Program, and LCMS World Relief. The campaign supports African churches and communities as they withstand HIV/AIDS, banish hunger, and build peace.

There is also the ELCA World Hunger Appeal, which promotes immediate relief for people in need, provides means for long-term development, and advocates for justice.

Lutheran Social Services in America is now the largest nonprofit provider of social services in the United States. It builds on the rich legacy of social ministry and health-care organizations. Their motto of "serving others following the example of our Lord Jesus" is lived out through refugee resettlement, mental-health services, adoption placement, transitional housing, extended care, and much more.

How do we maintain hope in the face of such overwhelming problems and not fall victim to compassion fatigue?

We begin by remembering that the God who sends us out into the world has also promised us the Holy Spirit to empower and guide us. We receive that Spirit as we worship together, fed by word and sacrament, strengthened by prayer.

We realize that we don't have to go it alone, and we don't have to do it all. We have the support of other Christians in the local congregation, in the synod, in the church-wide expression of the ELCA. Through the Division of Global Mission we are in part-nership with churches on every continent. Through our ecumenical relationships, we join with other Christian churches in this country and abroad.

We need to ground our action in the true source of our hope. When hope is tied to the outward look of things—the stability of the economy, the vitality of our congregation, the reality of terrorism, the uncertainty of our health—then precisely when we need hope most, it is often at its lowest ebb, unable to dispel our despair.

We have many things *for which* we hope. Yet far more important is the One *in whom* we hope—Jesus Christ, the light of the world. Jesus, who is "the same yesterday and today and forever" (Heb. 13:8), is also the one on the throne who says, "See, I am making all things new" (Rev. 21:5). In a changing world God is faithful.

QUESTIONS FOR DISCUSSION

1. Read these passages from the Old Testament prophets: Isaiah 58:6-12, Jeremiah 22:13-17, Amos 5:21-24. What is God saying about the mission of God's people?

2. What have you been doing to live out your baptismal covenant: to proclaim the good news of God in Christ through word and deed, to serve all people following the example of our Lord Jesus, to strive for justice and peace in all the earth?

3. Who are the people living in poverty in your community? your city? your township? county? state?

4. How does your congregation serve them? How might it serve better?

5. How does your congregation engage in striving for justice and peace in areas beyond your community?

6. What do you need in order to better fulfill that mission?

7. What did you find most interesting or helpful in this chapter?

You may wish to celebrate your discussion by singing a hymn:

LBW 415. "God of Grace and God of Glory"

LBW 423. "Lord, Whose Love in Humble Service"

LBW 562. "Lift Ev'ry Voice and Sing"

WOV 765. "Jesu, Jesu, Fill Us with Your Love"

WOV 722. "Hallelujah! We Sing Your Praises"

Close with this or another prayer:

Grant, O God, that your holy and life-giving Spirit may move every human heart, that the barriers which divide us may crumble, suspicions disappear, and hatreds cease, and that, with the divisions healed, we might live in justice and peace; through your Son, Jesus Christ our Lord (LBW, p. 42).

Chapter 4

AN EQUIPPING CHURCH

If we are to be an engaging church, answering the call of God to be engaged in the world as individuals and as congregations, we need to be an equipping church. If people are going to be engaged, they need more than motivational encouragements; they must be equipped with the understandings and skills required for effective and satisfactory action in the world.

We need to begin by equipping both lay people and clergy to discern their multiple callings from God. Our first calling is to faith and to life in community in Christ. We go on to hear the call of God in all areas of our lives. When I was elected bishop of the Saint Paul Area Synod, I said, "You need to know that as I accept your call, I do not cease to have other callings that I have already accepted. I will continue in my calling as a marriage partner with Ione, as a father to our six children, as a steward of God's creation and of my own life."

We hear God's call when, with the help of the community, we discern our gifts as individuals and as a congregation. Paul reminded the Corinthians and reminds us: "Now there are varieties of gifts but the same Spirit; and there are varieties of services, but the same Lord; and there are varieties of activities, but it is the same God who activates all of them in everyone. To each is given the manifestation of the Spirit for the common good" (1 Cor. 12:4-7).

We then identify the needs in the world around us and the point of intersection between those needs and our gifts. To use Frederick Buechner's phrase, we can look for the place where our deep gladness meets the world's deep need.

Congregations that begin by helping people discern their gifts often experience fresh energies and renewal in leadership. This is not to imply that God does not call us to develop new skills, stretch ourselves, take risks, but the first step might be recognizing and using the gifts we have been given.

Mapping the assets of our congregations and neighborhoods moves us from a preoccupation with what we lack and a possessiveness over what we have, to generously using our gifts for the sake of ministry and building sustainable communities.

An urban congregation in Detroit was struggling to have a viable ministry in an impoverished neighborhood. Members went door to door inviting people to describe their various gifts. At the end, all neighbors were invited to the church. On banners in the sanctuary were words describing the wide variety of gifts in the neighborhood. The evening became a celebration and the beginning of organizing these gifted neighbors.

Along with discerning gifts and assets, we need to equip people to live the faith in their daily lives—in the family, in the workplace, in the community. One of the great treasures of our Lutheran perspective on life and faith is our understanding of vocation, but we have sometimes allowed a chasm to develop between the language of Sunday worship and the Monday realities of the world in which we all live and work. People today are longing for bridges between the language of faith and the language of the workplace and community.

Bridges between faith and the world are being forged in the twenty-eight colleges and universities of the ELCA. This is the church in higher education, preparing and equipping Christian leaders, engaging in lively discourse and research, holding in tension faith and reason.

In the ELCA we also need to equip leaders for the church, both lay and clergy. When I ask bishops and other pastoral leaders what are the challenges they are facing, they often say, "We must raise up a new generation of leaders with a passion for ministry and mission." Our eight seminaries are preparing leaders for an apostolic church in an apostolic age, public leaders proclaiming the gospel, confronting principalities and powers, working for justice and peace.

As bishop of the Saint Paul Area Synod, I saw the great benefits that come from working with those trained in congregation-based organizing. We trained hundreds of members to do one-to-one visits in their congregations and neighborhoods. As they learned of people's hurts and hopes, they took the next step of gathering people to begin addressing issues in neighborhoods and to revitalize ministries. New leaders began to emerge, partnerships with neighboring congregations were formed, power to bring about change was experienced. Soon a metropolitan congregation-based organization was formed to find metropolitan solutions for metropolitan disparities. Pastors went to weeklong training to gain skills and confidence as community leaders.

We now have 2,259 congregations in the ELCA that are without a called pastor. I ask, "What would have to happen to reverse that situation? What if we had 2,000 new seminary graduates we could not immediately place into congregations? What if they could be sent out as missionaries to begin 2,000 *new* congregations?"

My dad was a traveling evangelist who was in a different congregation nearly every Sunday. I'd wait for him to come home and spend time with us. First he chose to go in his study and dictate letters to high school students he had met who had the potential gifts for leadership, encouraging them to consider a call to pastoral ministry. I've met pastors all over this church who say, "I never would have thought of being a pastor if your dad hadn't come to our church when I was in high school." We need to identify those who have the gifts for ministry, mentor them, encourage them, and provide the financial resources that will allow them to go to seminary.

We also have to find new ways and new models for congregations that cannot afford pastors. We've got to find ways to form leaders in these congregations and then expand that formation through lifelong learning. Fifty-four percent of congregations have fewer than 350 members. We need to continue to look for new ways to sustain word and sacrament ministries in these communities, as many synods are already doing.

As we think about equipping for leadership, we should also think beyond finding and training individual leaders and ask, "How does a congregation, as a body, exercise leadership in their community? How does the ELCA with 5.1 million people exercise collective leadership?"

Does the role of pastor need to change to make it more attractive or to prevent burnout?

We have to find ways for people to rediscover and celebrate what it means to be a pastor. People want their lives to count for something, and even people who feel a call to public ministry want to know that this is a meaningful vocation. If they hear only horror stories of conflict or stagnation or "clergy killers," they're not going to be drawn to congregational ministry. I believe that congregations centered on word and sacrament and mission will receive pastors as gifts from God and will attract people to this calling.

We have to strengthen the perception of pastoral ministry in a way that doesn't communicate that the only way to exercise leadership is by becoming a pastor, but we may have gone so far the other way that some of our most gifted young people don't even think of becoming pastors.

For those who have already accepted the call to pastoral ministry, we need to create communities in which they are sustained, nurtured, fed, and supported.

How can people take on more leadership roles in the church when so many people are overly busy and overburdened?

In our congregations we can ask, "Are we just adding more burdens to overburdened lives, more busyness to overly busy families?" We can look at what we are asking people to do. "Does this committee really have a purpose?

Is this meeting necessary? How are these activities helping this congregation or this community?"

Increasingly, neither men nor women are willing to come and do what they perceive as busy work. We need to look at our congregational life and ask, "Is there something going on for which people want and need to be equipped?"

Congregations with a clear sense of the mission to which God is calling have an easier time finding people who want to be involved. When we take the time to be clear together about the mission to which God is calling our congregation, we can do what is needed to get the work done— identifying gifts and organizing energies and resources.

QUESTIONS FOR DISCUSSION

1. Read 1 Corinthians 12:4-31. What gifts has God given you to be used in ministry in the world?

2. How do you hear the calling of God in your life?

3. Where is the place where your deep gladness meets the world's deep need?

4. How might your congregation, your faith community, help you carry out your callings in the world?

5. What is your congregation doing to discover and equip future leaders?

6. How does your congregation exercise leadership in your community?

7. What did you find most interesting or helpful in this chapter?

You may want to close your discussion by singing a hymn:

LBW 423. "Lord, Whose Love in Humble Service"

LBW 436. "All Who Love and Serve Your City"

LBW 469. "Lord of All Hopefulness, Lord of All Joy"

LBW 505. "Forth in Thy Name, O Lord, I Go"

WOV 755. "We All Are One in Mission"

Close with this or another prayer:

Almighty God, draw our hearts to you, guide our minds, fill our imaginations, control our wills, so that we may be wholly yours. Use us as you will, always to your glory and the welfare of your people; through our Lord and Savior Jesus Christ (LBW, p. 47).

Chapter 5

AN INVITING
CHURCH

It's been said that the average Lutheran invites someone to worship once every twenty-three years. If that's not bad enough, research also shows that it takes three invitations before the people invited come. That makes for sixty-nine years—and most of us don't have that much time!

Being an inviting church means inviting your neighbors, colleagues, and family members to come and hear the story of God's love in Christ. Most of us have come to the faith because someone else has brought us—parents brought us to the font, a friend invited us to Sunday school, a neighbor told us about the exciting things going on at her church. Having been invited into the church, we become those who invite others. We don't look to the evangelism committee to do it for us. It's the common task we all share—to be an inviting church.

I like the process of inviting that we see in John's Gospel. The process begins with a simple yet heartfelt invitation like that of the Samaritan woman: "Come and see a man who told me everything I have ever done!" (John 4:20). Seeing Jesus moves us into an ever-deepening relationship in which Jesus abides in us, and we in him. That abiding in Jesus is reflected in our love for one another.

There are many people who have never heard the story of Jesus, but there are also those who once knew it and have left it behind. We need to share with them the biblical invitation: "Return to the Lord, who is gracious and merciful, slow to anger, and abounding in steadfast love" (Joel 2:13). I especially wonder how we can share that invitation with young adults, many of whom have a significantly different culture, language, and music than older adults. Do we simply expect them to become like us, or are we willing to learn with and from them what it means to be followers of Christ?

What gets in the way of our inviting others to Christ?

Perhaps it is the fear that we may sound foolish. Even if that's the case, we can take comfort in Paul's words that "God decided, through the foolishness of our proclamation, to save those who believe" (1 Cor. 1:21).

Perhaps we've been so intimidated by the witnessing methods of some fundamentalists that we don't want to have anything to do with inviting people to Christ and into the community that bears his name.

Perhaps we've become lazy because the line between church and culture became so blurred. At one time everyone living in a community was expected to go to church, but our culture no longer automatically produces church members.

Have we accepted the cultural norm that what one believes is a matter of the heart and no one else's business? That was not Jesus' assumption when he invited his disciples to leave all and follow him.

It may be that we need conversation starters. In teaching a class on witnessing in daily life, I followed the example of a Chicago church. Each member was asked to wear a button that read: "Go ahead . . . ask me." During the week, people would respond, "Ask you what?", creating an opportunity to speak about one's faith and one's church. When I wore such a button home, it triggered a conversation with my own daughter! We need to remember and trust that the Holy Spirit will use our words, just as God has promised.

In the process of inviting, I think it's important that we put ourselves in the place of the guest, the stranger, the outsider. It may be helpful to visit other places of worship—other Christian churches or a Jewish or Muslim place of worship. Being more aware of what it feels like to be the outsider will make us better hosts, more sensitive to the stranger.

Even more fundamental than visiting other places of worship is remembering that we are all guests in God's house. Jesus Christ is our host, bidding us to come and dine at the table of his presence.

We need to ask questions about our hospitality toward those we have invited: Do we have greeters? Are our bulletins reader-friendly? Do we follow up with a call or visit? We need to look at our sermons, our Bible classes, our opportunities for service and ask, "Would a stranger want to come to this? Are people hearing the gospel, the good news of Jesus? Are they hearing and experiencing a word of grace?"

An example of hospitality is my mother, who belonged to Saint Anthony Park

Lutheran Church in St. Paul. Throughout her life, her rule was that she would not speak to people she knew on Sunday morning until she had greeted at least three people she did not know. If they were new to the area, she learned their names and addresses. Then, during the week, she went to their homes with a gift of chocolate chip cookies, thanking them for coming to church.

What first impressions do people have of your congregation? It is my hope that we as the ELCA are known as an inviting church, with each member bringing colleagues and classmates, family members and friends, even strangers, to hear the good news of God's love in Christ Jesus.

I hope that we are recognized as a church in which the proclamation of the word and celebration of the sacraments are central. May we be seen as a people who live out our Christian faith through our varied vocations, in acts of service, relentlessly pursuing justice and peace and steadfastly caring for God's creation.

When people see us, what is their first impression? That we are forgiven sinners singing praise and offering thanks to God? I believe so. That we are becoming more inclusive in our richly diverse culture? I trust so. That we are deepening our ecumenical relationships and expanding our global partnerships? I know so. That we are absolutely committed to ending hunger and being in ministry with people living in poverty? I pray so. That we are a Christ-centered, Spirit-filled, gospel-proclaiming, praying church in God's mission? It is so.

Is inviting people to church for Sunday worship the place to begin?

There need to be many doors through which one enters the community of the church. The front door of worship is one, but there are also side doors: day care, a support group for divorced people, Alcoholics Anonymous meetings, parenting classes, preschools, public advocacy for justice. We realize, of course, that it is through the means of grace that we are brought to faith.

People are hungry for community, for a place to belong, but it has to be a place where they sense something worthwhile is going on, where they can both receive and give.

I hear lots of talk these days in the church about color and race and sexual orientation, but little about class. Many of our congregations, especially the large suburban ones, are dominantly middle class. Does that make it hard for people living in poverty to be accepted there?

Absolutely. This is especially true for the hidden poor—the working poor of all races and ethnic groups. We do not identify people by their income, yet we often subtly shun or shame the poor.

It is tragic if we declare that God's love and forgiveness are given unconditionally in Christ Jesus, but at the same time convey the message that one must be of a certain economic means to be welcome in our church. That certainly would be the opposite of the example of Jesus. What a stir he created as he welcomed the outcast, sat at table with sinners, touched lepers, and spoke to a Samaritan woman in public.

May we be so bold in our inviting!

QUESTIONS FOR DISCUSSION

1. Read John 1:43-51. Have you ever invited anyone to church? If so, what happened? If not, what has prevented you?

2. Have you recently experienced worship in another denomination or religion? What was your experience?

3. What are the barriers to people coming to your Sunday worship service?

4. What would have to happen for the membership of your congregation to double? What would be good about that? What would be disturbing?

5. What are some "side doors" (other than Sunday worship) by which you could invite someone into your congregation?

6. Identify three people you know whom you could invite. Discuss your choices in your group. Invite one of your chosen people.

7. What did you find most interesting or helpful in this chapter?

You may want to conclude your discussion with a hymn:
LBW 381. "Hark, the Voice of Jesus Calling"
LBW 403. "Lord, Speak to Us, That We May Speak"

LBW 433. "The Church of Christ, in Every Age"

WOV 651. "Shine, Jesus, Shine"

WOV 712. "Listen, God Is Calling"

Close with this or another prayer:

Merciful Father, your kindness caused the light of the Gospel to shine among us. Extend your mercy now, we pray, to all the people of the world who do not have hope in Jesus Christ, that your salvation may be made known to them also and that all hearts would turn to you; through the same Jesus Christ, your Son our Lord (LBW, p. 45).

Chapter 6

A CONNECTING CHURCH

To be a witnessing, worshiping, engaging equipping, inviting church, we will also have to be a connecting church. We cannot be in isolation from the rest of the body of Christ. We need ligaments and circulatory and nervous systems to keep that body connected and flourishing because the body does not exist for its own sake but for the sake of the engagement of the gospel with the world.

In our worship we stand and confess; "We believe in one holy, catholic, and apostolic church." For all our individualism we say that, through God's word and work, we belong to a community in Christ that spans space and time. We belong to all Christians everywhere and throughout history.

The ELCA's commitment to ecumenism is rooted in Scripture. In Ephesians 4, Paul speaks of "one Lord, one faith, one baptism, one God and Father of all, who is above all and through all and in all" (vv. 5-6). Paul also speaks of the church as "one body in Christ" (Romans 12:5). In his high priestly prayer Jesus prayed for his disciples: "that they all may be one" (John 17:21).

Our commitment to ecumenism is also rooted in the context of our history. In 1991, the ELCA adopted a policy statement titled *Ecumenism: The Vision of the Evangelical Lutheran Church in America*. This includes a statement to which we are committed as members of this church:

"The unity of the church, as it is proclaimed in the Scriptures, is a gift and goal of God in Christ Jesus. Ecumenism is the joyous experience of the unity of Christ's people and the serious task of expressing that unity visibly and structurally to advance the proclamation of the Gospel for the blessing of humankind. Through participation in ecumenical activity, the Evangelical Lutheran Church in America seeks to be open in faith to the work of the Spirit, so as to manifest more fully oneness in Christ.

"To be ecumenical means to be committed to the oneness to which God calls the world in the saving gift of Jesus Christ. It also means to recognize the brokenness of the church in history and the call of God, especially in this century, to heal this disunity of Christ's people."

Although we in the ELCA share a commitment to manifest the unity we have in Christ, we do not always agree on how best to do that. I see three needs in ecumenism: one, the need to experience our unity in Christ; two, to more fully explore our unity; three, to more boldly express that unity in public witness. Let's look at each of these needs in turn.

First, we need to experience that unity locally, nationally, and globally. In Minnesota, we had a three-day conversation of Christians from many denominations and traditions, meeting in small groups simply to talk about the faith and the world in which we live as Christians. In our conversations, and especially as we joined in worship, we experienced both the richness of our diversity and a surprising community of faith.

Second, we need to explore our unity in conversation, to deepen and clarify it. This needs to be the work not just of theological experts who specialize in ecumenism, but of parish pastors and lay people as well. This process takes time. It includes the sustained work of theologians and members of congregations joining for "living room dialogues."

Third, we need to express our unity in public worship and witness, praying together, working together in disaster relief, refugee resettlement providing housing and food for the poor, and seeking for justice.

God has blessed us with a rich array of relationships with other Christians:

• at the personal level, among friends, relatives, and neighbors;

• at the community level, where we worship and work with other Christians—Lutheran, Catholic, Orthodox, Protestant, Evangelical;

• at the national level, through the churchwide expression of the ELCA, through the dozens of ways we cooperate with other denominations;

• at the global level, as we in the ELCA enter into partnerships with other Lutheran churches in the Lutheran World Federation and with national Lutheran churches through our Division for Global Mission. Through our membership in the National Council of Churches and the World Council of Churches, we are also workers together with other followers of Christ around the globe.

One of the great connections to the world is the companion synod and companion congregation programs. The Saint Paul Area Synod, for example, has learned what it means to be the church in the world through its partnership with the Iringa Diocese of the Evangelical Lutheran Church in Tanzania. We learned that congregations in Tanzania are expected to share the story of Jesus with neighbors, open clinics in the village, start schools, plant trees, and diversify agriculture.

We in the ELCA are also vitally interested in learning from members of the other world religions about their beliefs and practices. For example, at this time it is especially critical that we learn more about Islam and get to know Muslim people in our country and the world. Living in an increasingly pluralistic society invites us to greater clarity about what it means to be Lutheran Christians, even as we learn about others and join in building a more just world.

How can we move forward on issues like ecumenism without losing the connections we have with one another?

To guide us in these discussions we can ask some searching questions: What unites us and who unites us as a church body? How much uniformity does our unity demand? How much diversity does our unity permit? How do we manifest our unity in Christ? Our answers to those questions will help us move together to address our common concerns.

There are challenging issues ahead for us. The 2001 churchwide assembly has called for further study on sexuality. We will invite this church into conversation regarding God's mysterious, powerful gift of sexuality and the place of persons who are gay and lesbian in the life and ministry of this church.

My concern is that we undertake this process with integrity, that we keep the conversation rooted in our understanding of the word of God and our confessional and theological traditions, and in listening to one another for the leading of the Holy Spirit. Otherwise the anxiety over the divisions that we might experience will prevail over the sense of urgency for God's mission to which we are called.

As we engage in this study, we will have to hold it in tension with the fact that the churchwide assembly has also called us to develop a new evangelism strategy, a new strategy for Hispanic ministry, a new strategy for mission with Asian-Pacific people. We dare not neglect all these challenges by focusing on only one issue, important as it is. Let our conversation about ministry with gay and lesbian people be in the context of what it means to be the body of Christ in the world. Let us be sure it is a dialogue *with* persons who are gay and lesbian and not *about* them. Let it not exempt those of us who are heterosexual from dealing honestly with how *we* are stewards of the gift of sexuality. Let us see this discussion not as a problem but as an opportunity to witness to the love and grace and mercy of God.

I don't know what this study will conclude, but I do know that we belong to brothers and sisters in Christ by virtue of God's action in our lives in the waters of Baptism, before any of us knew what sexual orientation means, let alone what sexual orientation we have. So our discussion on these issues, as about all issues, will be among sisters and brothers in Christ.

Why should we in a local congregation care about an issue like ecumenical relationships? It seems remote from us.
For one thing, we can ask a bigger question than just "What do we get out of this?" We can look at every ecumenical agreement or

relationship not just in terms of what it can give us, but also as another way we have to make visible the unity we have in Christ.

These ecumenical agreements do help us in our work in the world. We can't do it all alone. By cooperating with other Christians we recognize one another as members of the same family, workers with us in the kingdom of God.

At the same time we can continue to appreciate the particularity of who we are as Lutherans. I grew up in a Lutheran home and attended a Lutheran college. I decided to study at an ecumenical seminary, but then returned to the Lutheran church. A significant factor in that return was the little word *and.* As part of my Lutheran heritage I believe that

- the creation is good *and* fallen;
- we are both saint *and* sinner;
- Jesus is human *and* divine, crucified *and* risen;
- the word is both law *and* gospel;
- we live in the kingdom of the left *and* the kingdom of the right;
- we are Lutherans *and* we are members of the holy catholic church, the one body of Christ.

I thank God for all the ways we are connecting with other Christians, not for the sake of the church, but for the sake of the gospel, for the sake of the world. This is not my church or your church. It is Christ's church. What a privilege it is to bear his mark on our brow, to bear his name into the world, and to serve him!

QUESTIONS FOR DISCUSSION

1. Read Jesus' prayer in John 17. What do you think he was envisioning for his followers?

2. What have been your most significant experiences of unity with other Christians?

3. How does your congregation express its unity with other Christians in your community?

4. What further opportunities for unity are open to you?

5. In what ways does your connection with the ELCA aid the ministry of your congregation?

6. How much uniformity does our unity in the ELCA demand? How much diversity does it allow?

7. How can we discuss tough issues in the church without alienating one another?

8. What did you find most interesting or helpful in this chapter?

Close your discussion by singing a hymn like one of these:

LBW 126. "Where Charity and Love Prevail"

LBW 359. "In Christ There Is No East or West"

LBW 369. "The Church's One Foundation"

WOV 650. "We Are Marching in the Light of God"

WOV 748. "Bind Us Together"

WOV 773. "Send Me, Jesus"

Close with this or another prayer:

Gracious Father, we pray for your holy catholic church. Fill it with all truth and peace. Where it is corrupt, purify it; where it is in error, direct it; where in anything it is amiss, reform it; where it is right, strengthen it; where it is in need, provide for it; where it is divided, reunite it; for the sake of Jesus Christ, your Son our Savior (LBW, p. 45).

Chapter 7

A CHANGING CHURCH

The Lutheran church began as a reforming movement in the Roman Catholic Church. Luther did not set out to establish a new church, but to reform the existing church for the sake of the gospel, contending that the church must be *semper reformanda,* always reforming. We believe that the church is always being re-formed by the Holy Spirit working through the gospel. How do we live out that dynamic vision—both as individuals and as a church?

It would be tragic if the Lutheran church, born as an agent of change, were to resist change. We need to be open to change—not for the sake of change, but for the gospel and the work that God is calling us to do in the world.

For perspective, we can look again at the church in the Book of Acts. There we see a church in constant change. We go from seeing thousands converted in one day, to Stephen being martyred, to people orienting their daily life around prayer, sharing bread, and holding all things in common. We see the early church dealing with hard controversial divisive questions: Do you have to be Jewish to be a Christian? Can the Gentiles be accepted as they are? What is our responsibility to the poor in Jerusalem? They confronted dramatic change in basic presuppositions, in behavior, in communal life—change that ultimately led to death for some but life for others. In the midst of all that change, the early Christians remained grounded in certain basic realities: one Lord, one faith, one baptism.

We need to be a church grounded in the Scripture, the Lutheran Confessions, theology, and the liturgy. At the same time we need to be a church engaged in analysis of the culture in which we live and in strategic planning and thinking. In a dynamic world, we will be faithful yet changing. We are a missionary church in a missionary context with a growing diversity in our population and culture.

Look at the 2000 U. S. Census data and compare it with the demographics of the ELCA. There are twelve million Asians in the United States; we have twenty-two thousand in the ELCA. Four hundred thousand Asians are coming to the United States. every year; last year the Asian population in the ELCA declined by one hundred.

In 1988, the year the ELCA was formed, there were forty-eight thousand African-Americans in our church. Now there are fifty-two thousand—a gain of four thousand in twelve years.

In 1988, there were twenty-two thousand Hispanic-Americans in the ELCA. In 2000, there were thirty-six thousand.

If we don't become a changing church, we will be simply a museum piece in the religious history of the American people. Historians will say there was once an immigrant people who came from Europe, bringing with them their faith as Lutheran Christians, but they couldn't adapt to a changing, diverse, pluralistic culture. That's our fate unless we also become a changing church in a changing culture.

As a missionary church in a missionary context, we have to be willing to be changed by the new people who come into our churches. I believe that such changes will not occur unless we are willing to confront the racism in our lives and institutions. If we think we are going to go out into a pluralistic context and invite people of color to join us and be like us, we will not succeed—nor should we. But we are a Pentecost people, each speaking the mighty acts of God in our own tongue, hearing and understanding one another, going into the world to share that story.

As a changing church, we will need to let go of what we have been in order to become a more diverse community that reflects the hues and cultural richness that now exist in our land. Our unity in Christ is not inconsistent with an appreciation for our diversity. The Apostle Paul helps us understand that when he describes the church as the body of Christ.

Isn't this concern for diversity primarily an urban issue? What about the many ELCA churches in rural areas?

The issues surrounding diversity may not be as readily apparent in rural areas, but there too we find the Native American population and a growing number of Latinos and Asians. There too we have the poor. Rural poverty is more hidden but just as real, particularly among the working poor.

Rural communities are not static. They are facing the loss of farms, unplanned urban sprawl, the degradation of the land, the decline of small towns. The Search Institute of Minneapolis has documented that at-risk behaviors among young people—including drug and alcohol abuse, reckless driving, and unwanted pregnancies—are as big a problem in rural areas as in our urban centers.

Churches in rural areas are providing the leadership needed for healthy change, for the survival of communities and the rural economy, for land stewardship, and for the survival of these rural congregations.

Is there a danger that we will pursue change just for the sake of change?

Sure, just as there is the danger that we will keep things the same just for the sake of keeping them the same. Not all change is good; not all change is progress. Here is another place where we need to practice discernment. The change that is needed is the change that grows out of our call to be a witnessing, worshiping, engaging, equipping, inviting church in the world. It is not change for the sake of change, but change for the sake of the gospel.

How does the church change without self-destructing?

I believe that change should be seen as a by-product rather than as a goal. When a congregation is united around a conviction that we are forgiven sinners joined to God's mission in and for the sake of the world, then change is not as threatening.

I saw this in the churches of St. Paul, where there was impetus for change as we discerned our call to mission. People were underfed, underhoused, not paid a living wage, and they were not able to solve these problems by themselves. In order to engage these issues, we developed a strong congregation-based ecumenical organization called ISAIAH, which trained leaders to reach out to their neighborhoods and congregations. These leaders were committed to enriching worship, expanding outreach, and developing partnerships with other congregations in youth ministry.

I can share another example from the life of the Saint Paul Area Synod. We had quite an elaborate and somewhat cumbersome bureaucracy of boards and committees and task forces. In order to get past business as usual, we had to clear the decks and spend a year in prayer and conversation. If I had said, "We're going to change this synod and restructure it," that would have created a lot of defensiveness. First we had to go through a process of discernment about what God might be calling us to do.

We invited all our boards and committees and task forces to meet at Luther Seminary for a dinner. We had a Bible study on the jubilee texts of the Old and New Testaments. We blew a ram's horn, declaring a jubilee year: committees and boards were told they were free not to meet, except for a few essential ones. Instead, we would spend a year in conversation and prayer about what God could possibly do with 165,000 baptized Christians in 120 congregations, working together. The result was a call to the synod to be a catalyst, asking other churches to join us in a threefold task: raising ten thousand leaders with a vision for mission, local and global; extending to every person living in the synod area an invitation to hear the story of Jesus; and working together so that no one in the synod area would be forced to live in poverty. The last event I attended as synod bishop was the training of more than three hundred visitors, who went into the city of St. Paul and the suburbs, visiting households, listening to hurts and hopes, and inviting people to worship.

That was bold thinking, Pentecost thinking. We ordered synod life around these three goals and created leadership teams to move them toward reality. Most of the other committees and task forces were never reconstituted. All this happened only when we took the time for prayer and conversation around the questions, "What do you think God could do here? What difference could God make in the church and the world by virtue of our working together?"

If we approach change from the standpoint of covering our deficiencies rather than calling forth our gifts, we'll face resistance. The congregations I visited that were anxiety-driven or focused on what they lacked became angry at their pastor and one another. It was very different for congregations that began by identifying their gifts or assets. Change then came on the basis of the grace God had shown people in their community.

If we operate out of a mindset of scarcity, we become anxious, distrustful, and unneighborly, but if we trust in the abundance of God's grace and the gifts God has given this community, we can move ahead and embrace change for the sake of mission.

One of the ways we need to change is in our patterns of giving. That the average ELCA member gives less than two percent of his or her income to the church is simply not acceptable. I believe that a church that bears the eight marks described in this book, and that trusts in the abundance of God's grace and gifts, will experience growth in faith, membership, and the generous giving of money and time. As a giving and growing church, we will be faithful to the mission to which God is calling us.

QUESTIONS FOR DISCUSSION

1. How has your faith changed from the time you were a child?

2. How has your congregation changed in the past twenty years?

3. Do you see these changes as positive or negative? Why?

4. How is the community in which your church is located changing?

5. How might your church need to change to meet these changes?

6. What are the biggest barriers to change in your congregation? How might they be overcome?

7. What changes would you most like to see in the churchwide expression of the ELCA, as a denomination?

8. What did you find most interesting or helpful in this chapter?

You may want to close your discussion by singing a hymn like one of these:
LBW 459. "O Holy Spirit, Enter In"
LBW 393. "Rise Shine, You People"
LBW 476. "Have No Fear, Little Flock"
WOV 755. "We All Are One in Mission"
WOV 722. "Hallelujah! We Sing Your Praises"
WOV 756. "Lord, You Gave the Great Commission"

Close with this or another prayer:
O God, you made us in your own image and redeemed us through Jesus your Son. Look with compassion on the whole human family; take away the arrogance and hatred which infect our hearts; break down the walls that separate us; unite us in bonds of love; and through our struggle and confusion, work to accomplish your purposes on earth; that, in your good time, all nations and races may serve you in harmony around your heavenly throne; through Jesus Christ our Lord (LBW, p. 44).

Chapter 8

A PRAYING CHURCH

I have saved prayer for the last chapter of this little book, not because it is least important, but because it undergirds everything else that we do. If everything else we have discussed in this book is going to become reality, then we will have to be a praying church.

The basic question is, How do we stay renewed for our mission in the world? We simply can't do it unless we are daily in the word, regularly at the Lord's table, faithfully among the gathered community, and in the presence of God in personal and corporate prayer.

One of the clearest ways we testify to our faith is through the witnessing of our public prayer.

An essential element of our worshiping together is prayer, both the silent adoration of the heart and our intercession, bringing one another and the world before the throne of God's grace.

Our engaging in the world is guided and empowered by prayer.

A vital aspect of our equipping is teaching the people of the church—children, youth, adults, seniors—to pray. We need parish pastors and lay teachers who equip people for prayerful lives. Our congregations should be schools of prayer.

Our inviting can be directed by prayer as we begin to actively invite others into the praying community.

Our connecting with other Christians is based in prayer. Prayer is where we concretely experience our unity in Christ.

Our changing will be guided by prayer, especially the prayer of discernment, as we discover together the ways in which our churches can be renewed and empowered for mission in the world, as we seek a vision of what God wants to do with us and through us.

We will be a praying church.

As I've begun to travel around the church, I am so heartened by the people who say to me, "We are praying for you and for this church." It's a wonderful word of promise.

Dietrich Bonhoeffer wrote: "A Christian community either lives by the intercessory prayers of its members for one another, or the community will be destroyed. I can no longer condemn or hate other Christians for whom I pray. In intercessory prayer the face that may have been strange and intolerable to me is transformed into the face of one for whom Christ died, the face of a pardoned sinner. That is a blessed discovery for the Christian who is beginning to offer intercessory prayer for others. As far as we are concerned, there is no dislike, no personal tension, no disunity or strife, that cannot be overcome by intercessory prayer. Intercessory prayer is the purifying bath into which the individual and the community must enter every day" (p. 90).

Our Saint Paul Synod staff accepted intercession as a significant part of our calling. Every Wednesday we spent time in prayer for the synod and its people. We divided up the synod into groups, and we would send cards to congregations and rostered leaders, saying, "This Wednesday we will be praying for you. Do you have any special concern about that which we should pray?" People responded with requests and with gratitude.

Prayer is especially necessary for leaders in the church—both lay and clergy. All Christians, but especially leaders in the church, need to do inner work, involving such practices as spiritual reading, journaling, meditation, and prayer. Such inner work is just as important and real as the outer work of teaching, healing, serving, and doing justice. Indeed, if our inner work is not done faithfully, our outer work will suffer.

This inner work, while personal, is not private. We do it not as lone individuals, but as members of a worshiping community rooted in word and sacrament. We look to one another for support and correction. We seek through our inner work to be strengthened for the work in the world to which God has called us.

How did you learn to pray?

At our family table, prayer was a part of every meal. We didn't just recite memorized prayers or read written prayers. Everyone, including the children, was expected to pray aloud, freely expressing our thoughts and needs to God. We prayed, and we sang hymns. My parents did a lot of entertaining. There was always fabulous food and lively conversation, but the evening always ended with singing and praying.

One challenge we have is to recover

something of Luther's idea that the home should be the center of religious education and worship. Christian education in the Sunday school or church school is important, but it can never substitute for the spiritual life in the home, with parents and children gathered around the word and prayer.

My spiritual director, Bill Smith, taught me to ask before I close my eyes at night, "In whose face today did I see the face of Christ?" This is a gathering of the experiences of the day, a collecting of thoughts in the presence of God.

My life includes personal prayer, but I also need communal prayer, especially because I'm an extrovert. In the past I had a group of six clergy that met to pray together regularly. This was energizing for me, but it also provided me with accountability. I had spiritual friends who would hold me to my spiritual disciplines.

How can we find time in our busy lives for prayer?

Bill Smith also has helped me see that prayer is not one more thing I have to do every day, but it is simply placing myself consciously and intentionally in the presence of God. He reminded me of the teaching of Brother Lawrence: "Do not seek God everywhere, but find God everywhere. In the midst of whatever you're doing, keep a little interior glance to the Spirit, who is praying in you."

I think there is a rediscovery in our day of the need for the contemplative life, the inner life, the care of the soul.

People are also reclaiming sabbath, or a rhythm of life that includes rest and renewal and refreshment. If my days don't have this ebb and flow, I end up being less than human. I need to include time for what is really re-creative for me, like time in nature, time for music and reading.

Each person has to discover for himself or herself how to build in some time for solitude, reflection, simply being in the presence of God. If, like many people, we have busy, overloaded lives, the sabbath time may help us discern what God is calling us to do and be and of what we need to let go.

We need both prayer in the gathered community and prayer alone in the presence of God. I like the way Dietrich Bonhoeffer balanced the need for solitude and community. In *Life Together* he wrote: "Only as we stand within the community can we be alone, and only those who are alone can live in community. Both belong together. Only in the community do we learn to be properly alone; and only in being alone do we learn to live properly in the community. It is not as if the one preceded the other; rather both begin at the same time, namely, with the call of Jesus Christ" (p. 83).

QUESTIONS FOR DISCUSSION

1. Jesus' disciples asked him, "Lord, teach us to pray." How did you learn to pray? Who were your teachers? How did they teach you?

2. How is prayer a part of your life now? How would you describe your own "inner work"?

3. Have you even been on the receiving end of intercessory prayer?

4. In what ways is your congregation a praying church?

5. How could your congregation help you be more faithful in prayer?

6. What is sabbath time for you?

7. What did you find most interesting or helpful in this chapter?

Conclude your discussion with a hymn like one of these:

LBW 439. "What a Friend We Have in Jesus"

LBW 440. "Christians, While on Earth Abiding"

LBW 444. "With the Lord Begin Your Task"

WOV 773. "Send Me, Jesus"

WOV 783. "Seek Ye First the Kingdom of God"

Close with this or another prayer:

Almighty God, you have given us grace at this time with one accord to make our common supplication to you, and you have promised through your well-beloved Son that when two or three are gathered together in his name, you will be in the midst of them. Fulfill now, O Lord, our desires and petitions as may be best for us, granting us, in this world, knowledge of your truth and, in the age to come, life everlasting (LBW, p. 48).

BIBLIOGRAPHY

Bonhoeffer, Dietrich. *Life Together,
Prayerbook of the Bible.* Minneapolis:
Fortress, 1996.

Jüngel, Eberhard. *Justification: The Heart of
the Christian Faith.* Edinburgh & New
York: T & T Clark, 2001.

Sittler, Joseph. *Gravity and Grace: Reflections
and Provocations.* Minneapolis: Augsburg,
1986.

ADDITIONAL RESOURCES

The ELCA Web site (www.elca.org) includes
a great deal of materials and information on
the themes discussed in this book. See especially "Resources" and "Call to Discipleship."

Augsburg Fortress, Publishers, also offers
many books and other resources on these
themes. See www.augsburgfortress.org for
more information.

ABOUT THE AUTHOR

In August 2001, the Evangelical Lutheran Church in America elected the Rev. Mark S. Hanson its third presiding bishop to serve a six-year term beginning November 1, 2001.

Born in Minneapolis in 1946, Hanson graduated from Minnehaha Academy in 1964 and Augsburg College in 1968. He was a Rockefeller Fellow at Union Theological Seminary and received his Master of Divinity degree from there in 1972. He attended Luther Seminary, St. Paul, in 1973-74 and was a Merrill Fellow at Harvard University Divinity School in 1979.

Ordained in 1974, Hanson served as pastor of Prince of Glory Lutheran Church, Minneapolis, 1973-79; Edina Community Lutheran Church, 1979-88; and University Lutheran Church of Hope, Minneapolis, 1988-1995. He began serving as bishop of the Saint Paul Area Synod of the ELCA in 1995, and had been reelected to a second term as synodical bishop prior to his election as presiding bishop.

Bishop Hanson is married to Ione (Agrimson) Hanson. They are the parents of Aaron, Alyssa, Rachel, Ezra, Isaac, and Elizabeth, and grandparents to Naomi.